JOAN *of* ARC

ENGLAND

ENGLISH

Cherbourg

BRITTANY   MAI

Loire

POIT

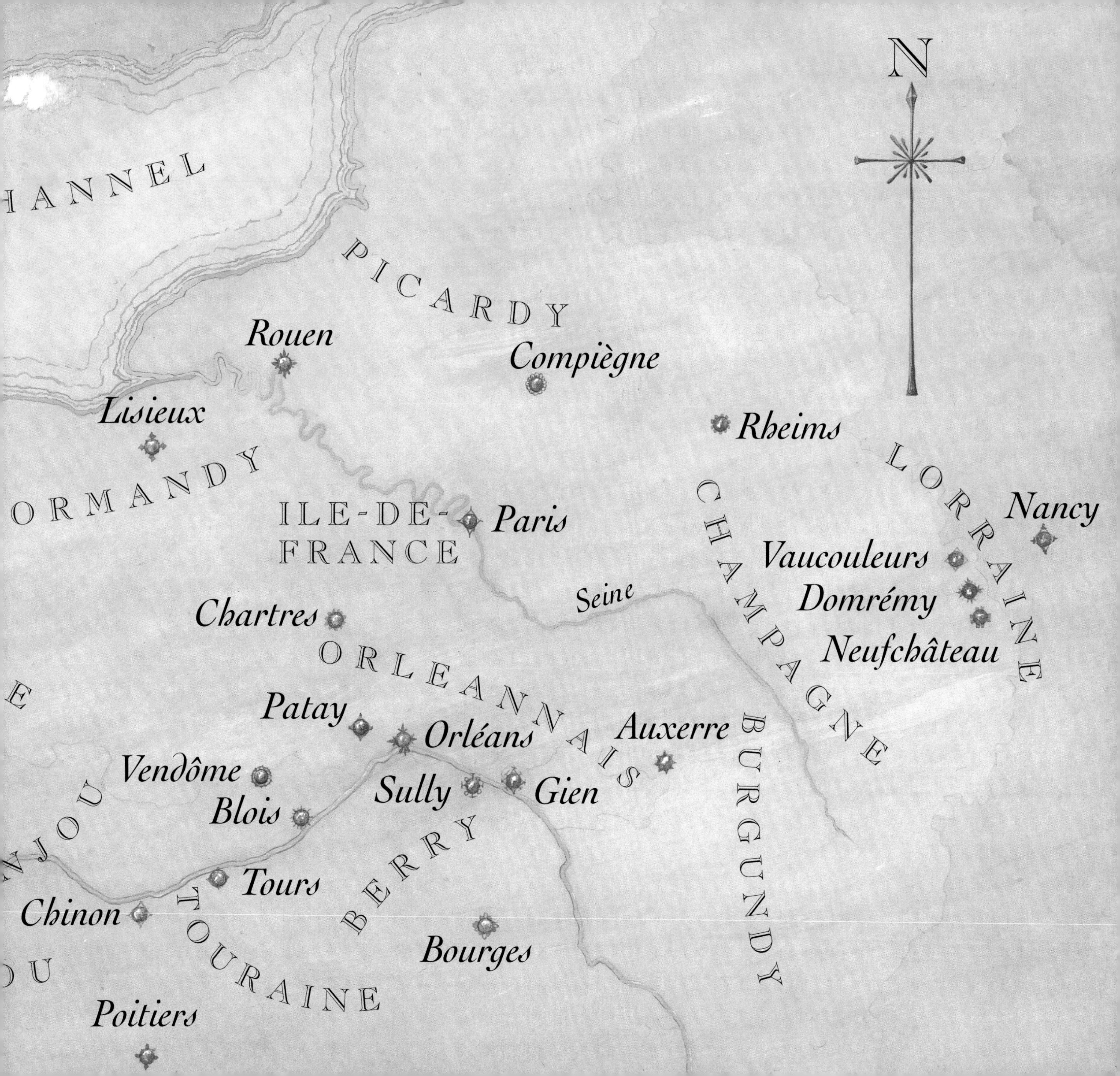

N

CHANNEL

PICARDY

Rouen

Compiègne

Lisieux

Rheims

LORRAINE

NORMANDY

ILE-DE-
FRANCE

Paris

Nancy

Vaucouleurs

CHAMPAGNE

Seine

Domrémy

Chartres

Neufchâteau

ORLEANNAIS

Patay

Orléans

Auxerre

Vendôme

Sully

Gien

BURGUNDY

Blois

Tours

BERRY

Chinon

Bourges

TOURAINE

ANJOU

Poitiers

Josephine Poole

JOAN OF ARC

Illustrated by Angela Barrett

Research by Vincent Helyar

Dragonfly Books® 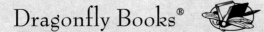 Alfred A. Knopf • New York

THIS IS A TRUE STORY. It happened over 500 years ago, in France.

The French King was in great danger. His cousin, the Duke of Burgundy, wanted the throne for himself, and had persuaded England to fight with him.

English ships set sail for France. English lords and soldiers captured many cities that belonged to the young French King. It looked as if he would be driven out, and he hadn't even been properly crowned.

Deep in the country, there lived a girl called Joan. She was a farmer's daughter. She helped her mother in the house, and worked in the fields with her brothers. Her father was mayor of the village where they lived.

ONE summer day, when Joan was alone in the garden, the air around her turned very clear and bright—much brighter than the sun could make it. While she was wondering what could be happening, she heard voices. They were talking to her.

She was afraid at first, until she understood that these were voices from Heaven. As she listened, she was full of happiness. She had never felt so happy.

When the Voices stopped and the heavenly light paled to sunshine, she cried because they had gone away.

Joan was thirteen when this happened. During the next four years, the Voices often spoke to her, but she never told anyone about them. To hear them was more important to her than anything in the world, although sometimes, when they spoke of the fighting in France, they made her cry.

As time passed, her heart was filled with a great will and desire that her King should have his kingdom.

ORLÉANS was one of the most important cities in France. Now it was surrounded by English soldiers, battering it with their cannons. Soon they would take it by storm.

The people inside the city prayed for an army to defend them. But no one came.

Far away, the Voices spoke to Joan. They told her that God had chosen her to save Orléans. After that, she must take the King of France to Rheims to be crowned.

Joan believed everything that the heavenly Voices said. She knew they came from God. If she did as she was told, nothing on earth would be strong enough to stop her.

JOAN needed an army to defeat the English. She had to see the King, but he was far away. So she put on her best red dress and left home, without telling anyone what she was going to do. She walked to the nearest town and asked for the Captain of the garrison there. She told him that God had chosen her to save Orléans, and asked him to arrange her journey to the King.

The Captain burst out laughing, and made fun of her. But she came back, and back again, until he finally agreed to help her.

He gave her a horse and four guards. She cut her hair and dressed like a man so that she could travel more safely. Now she was ready to start.

Everyone living in the town came to the gate to watch her ride out of sight.

STORIES about this country girl had already reached the King. When he heard she was coming, he took off his crown and dressed like one of his lords. This was to test her—if she really had supernatural powers, she surely would know which of all the lords was the King!

That evening, Joan arrived at the castle. The Great Hall was full of people, and ablaze with light. She went straight up to the true King and bowed. "God give you life, gentle King," she said.

"I am not the King, Joan," he said. He pointed to a friend. "There is the King."

"By God, gentle Prince, it is you and none other," said Joan.

Later, in private, she told him what the Voices had said—that she must free Orléans and take him to Rheims to be crowned.

THE King knew that only a miracle could save him from his enemies. But—Joan was such an ordinary girl! Besides, suppose her power didn't come from God? Suppose she was a witch!

He couldn't make up his mind. But Joan knew what would happen. There was no time to waste—she learned to gallop a war-horse and use a lance.

And at last her orders came.

Orléans was buzzing with rumors. God was sending a maiden with miraculous powers! She could see into the future! Saints came down from Heaven to talk to her! She was bringing food and soldiers to Orléans!

It was true. A convoy of wagons was on its way, and Joan rode in front with the captains.

That night, Joan rode into the city by the back gate. The narrow streets were crammed with people, carrying torches, cheering and rejoicing, and pressing forward to touch her.

And as they jostled against her, a flaring torch caught the pennant of her standard and set it alight. But spurring her horse, she turned him quickly and gently so that she could put out the fire. Everyone who saw it marveled at her horsemanship.

THE next evening, Joan went out on the bridge in front of the city. From there she could see the great multitude of English soldiers camped just across the river. But she had in her heart what the Voices had said. She knew that when the battle came, she would win it, and out of pity for the English, she shouted that if they surrendered, their lives would be saved.

"Peasant!" they yelled. "Take care we don't catch you! We'll burn you if we do!"

That made her angry, and she stormed back into the city.

Joan needed more soldiers before she could take on the full force of the English. When they came, she told her priest, "You must get up early tomorrow, and keep close to me all day. For tomorrow I shall have much to do, more than I ever had, and tomorrow blood will flow out of my body above my breast."

THE next morning, Joan rode out of Orléans with every soldier she had, and every man and boy strong enough to hold a sword or throw a stone. For the English army was huge, and very powerful. William Glasdale, or "Classidas" as the French called him, commanded it. And the fighting began.

Very soon, an arrow hit her, so that she bled. She was frightened and cried bitterly. Somebody ran up with a healing charm, but she would not have it. She undid her armor and stanched the wound herself, and then went on fighting.

The battle dragged on. Toward sunset, the Captain of Orléans decided that his men had had enough. He wanted to sound the trumpets to order them back into the city.

Joan begged him to wait just a little. Then she rode alone into a desolate vineyard. When she had prayed, she galloped back, seized her standard, and leapt upon the parapet of the trench. "It is all yours!" she shouted. "Go! Go!"

THE hearts of the French thrilled at the sight, but when the English saw Joan, they were overcome with terror. Several hundred of them crammed the bridge, trying to get back across the river. In the panic, nearly all of them perished.

Then Joan shouted, "Classidas, Classidas, surrender, surrender to the King of Heaven. You called me names, but I take pity on your soul, and on your people's!" But Glasdale, all armed as he was from head to feet, tumbled into the river and was drowned. And Joan wept for pity of him, and of all who died that day.

So the triumphant French went back into Orléans, while all the bells pealed for joy. But Joan was taken to her lodging. The surgeon dressed her wound with olive oil and lard, and afterward she ate four or five pieces of toast, with a little wine diluted in water, which she drank from a silver cup. This was the only food and drink she had that day.

THE next morning, the English lined up as if they meant to attack. Then Joan came out to face them, with many valiant soldiers and citizens. The French and the English stared at each other for an hour, but nobody started a fight. At last, the English marched away along the river.

Then Joan rode back into the city. And everyone thanked God, and praised Him, because it pleased Him that a pure maid had driven out the King's enemies.

The siege of Orléans was over. Now Joan had to take the King to Rheims to be crowned—but that part of the country was still in enemy hands. She rode ahead to clear the way. Her armor shone like silver, and she carried a little ax. A mighty host of captains and soldiers went with her—for now everyone wanted to fight with her, for France and the King.

The English believed that Joan was a witch, whose power came from the devil. But the French called her Joan the Maid, Daughter of God. People had seen clouds of white butterflies rising from her standard. They believed God commanded her through the Voices, saying, "Daughter of God, go, go, I shall be at your right hand, go!" Joan simply did what God told her to do, and nothing, nobody could prevent her.

When the people of Rheims saw the King coming, they ran out to welcome him. The next day, he was crowned in the cathedral with great splendor. But when Joan knelt in front of him, her eyes were full of tears. She could not forget how many brave men had died for her gentle prince.

Now Joan's work was done, and she should have gone home to the country. But her captains wanted her to stay with them so that they could win more battles together.

News came that the town of Compiègne was surrounded. The citizens said they would sooner die than surrender. Joan could not bear to leave them to their fate, although the Voices warned her that if she went, she would be taken prisoner.

She led a little army to Compiègne, and threading their way around the enemy camp by night, they slipped into the town. When morning came, they rode out to battle. But the Captain of Compiègne did not believe that such a small army could save them. As soon as Joan and her soldiers had gone, he ordered the drawbridge to be raised and the great gates locked. So the valiant French force was cut off.

They were hopelessly outnumbered. Joan was easy to recognize from the tunic she was wearing over her armor. A rough soldier dragged her from her horse.

JOAN was imprisoned in a castle that stood in the middle of a forest. Her lonely cell was high up in a tower. Alas, what sad thoughts tormented her! So many brave souls gone—she herself would willingly have given up her life for her King! Why didn't he help her now? What would become of her?

In fact, the French King had made a secret truce with his treacherous cousin, the Duke of Burgundy, and with the English—and Joan was part of the bargain.

Desperate with grief and anxiety, Joan said her prayers and jumped out of the window. She was caught at once and taken back—so bruised that she could neither eat nor drink for two days. During that dreadful time, St. Michael and his angels visited her, to comfort her. The Archangel was so beautiful, so kind, that she wept bitterly when he left her, because she could not go back with him to Heaven.

At last she was taken to Rouen for her trial. She was now in English hands, and the English needed to get rid of her, because to ordinary people, Joan was a heroine and a saint. A special court was set up to accuse her of heresy—pretending to hear heavenly voices, pretending to talk with saints and even see them. The punishment for heresy was death.

CAUCHON, the wicked Bishop of Beauvais, was waiting for Joan. He had been paid by the English to make sure that the trial went against her. He thought he could easily confuse the country girl, but he was wrong. She was not afraid of him. She had a warning for him. "You say you are my judge. Consider well what you are about, for in truth I am sent from God, and you are putting yourself in great danger."

Now Joan was kept in the prison of Rouen castle, cruelly chained to her bed. She was questioned for hours at a time, but she answered so fearlessly that no one could make her falter.

Still, she was doomed. She was condemned as a heretic, and sentenced to death by burning.

The Voices said, "Take all in good part, do not complain over thy martyrdom. By it thou shalt come at last to the Kingdom of Paradise."

The English carried out the sentence. But it was an Englishman who, at the last, made her a little cross of wood, which she kissed and hid inside her clothes. So she died by fire, and the ashes of her body were thrown into the river.

B̲ᴜᴛ that was not the end. A saint is like a star.
A star and a saint shine forever.

Chronology

1412?		Joan is born at Domrémy to Isabelle and Jacques d'Arc
1415		Henry V of England defeats the French at Agincourt
1420		Henry V marries Catherine, daughter of Charles VI of France
1422		Death of Henry V
		Death of Charles VI
		Dauphin takes the title Charles VII, King of France
1423		Treaty of Amiens between the Duke of Bedford and the Duke of Burgundy
		Submission of Normandy to the English
1424?		St. Michael the Archangel first speaks to Joan in the garden at Domrémy
		St. Catherine and St. Margaret also speak to her
1428	*May*	Joan's first visit to Vaucouleurs to see the Captain, Baudricourt
	October 12	Orléans besieged by the English and Burgundians
1429	*February*	Joan goes to Chinon to meet the Dauphin
	April 29	Joan enters Orléans
	May 8	Deliverance of Orléans
	June 29	Royal army leaves for Rheims through enemy territory via Auxerre, Troyés, and Châlons
	July 17	Consecration of the King, Charles VII, at Rheims
	September	Unsuccessful assault on Paris
		Charles VII disperses his army
		Joan raises a small army
	November	Unsuccessful assault on La Charité-sur-Lare
		Charles VII ennobles Joan's family, but is negotiating with the Duke of Burgundy
1430	*May*	Siege of Compiègne by the Burgundians
		Joan takes a small force to the rescue
	May 23	Joan is taken prisoner
	December 23	Joan is taken to Rouen, then the capital of English Normandy
1431	*January 9*	Joan's trial begins
	May 30	Joan is burned at the stake in the Old Market Square in Rouen
1435	*September 21*	Treaty of Arras between France and Burgundy
1436		Uprising in Paris
1437	*November*	Charles VII enters Paris
1449		Uprising in Rouen
	November	Charles VII enters Rouen
1450	*February 15*	Letter from Charles VII orders an inquiry into Joan's trial
	March	First inquiry when witnesses are called and heard
1452	*May*	Ecclesiastical inquiry into the case of Joan
1455	*June*	The Pope allows Isabelle, her mother, to undertake the process of Joan's rehabilitation
1456	*July*	Rehabilitation of Joan in the Archbishop's palace at Rouen
1920	*May 16*	Joan is canonized

DRAGONFLY BOOKS® PUBLISHED BY ALFRED A. KNOPF, INC.

www.randomhouse.com/kids

Library of Congress Cataloging-in-Publication Data
Poole, Josephine.
Joan of Arc / by Josephine Poole ; illustrated by Angela Barrett.
p.   cm.
Summary: A biography of the fifteenth-century peasant girl who led a French army to victory against the English,
witnessed the crowning of Charles VII, and was later burned at the stake for witchcraft.
1. Joan, of Arc, Saint, 1412–1431—Pictorial works—Juvenile literature.
2. Christian women saints—France—Biography—Pictorial works—Juvenile literature. 3. France—
History—Charles VII, 1422–1461—Pictorial works—Juvenile literature. 4. Hundred Years' War,
1339–1453—Pictorial works—Juvenile literature. [1. Joan, of Arc, Saint, 1412–1431. 2. Saints.
3. Women—Biography. 4. France—History—Charles VII, 1422–1461.]
I. Barrett, Angela, ill. II. Title.
DC103.5.P66   1998
940'.026'092—dc21
[B]
97-46667

ISBN 0-679-89041-6 (trade)
0-679-99041-0 (lib. bdg.)
0-375-80355-6 (pbk.)

First Dragonfly Books® edition: August 2000

Printed in Singapore
10 9 8 7 6 5 4 3 2 1

ENGLAND

ENGLISH

Cherbourg

BRITTANY

MAI

Loire

POIT

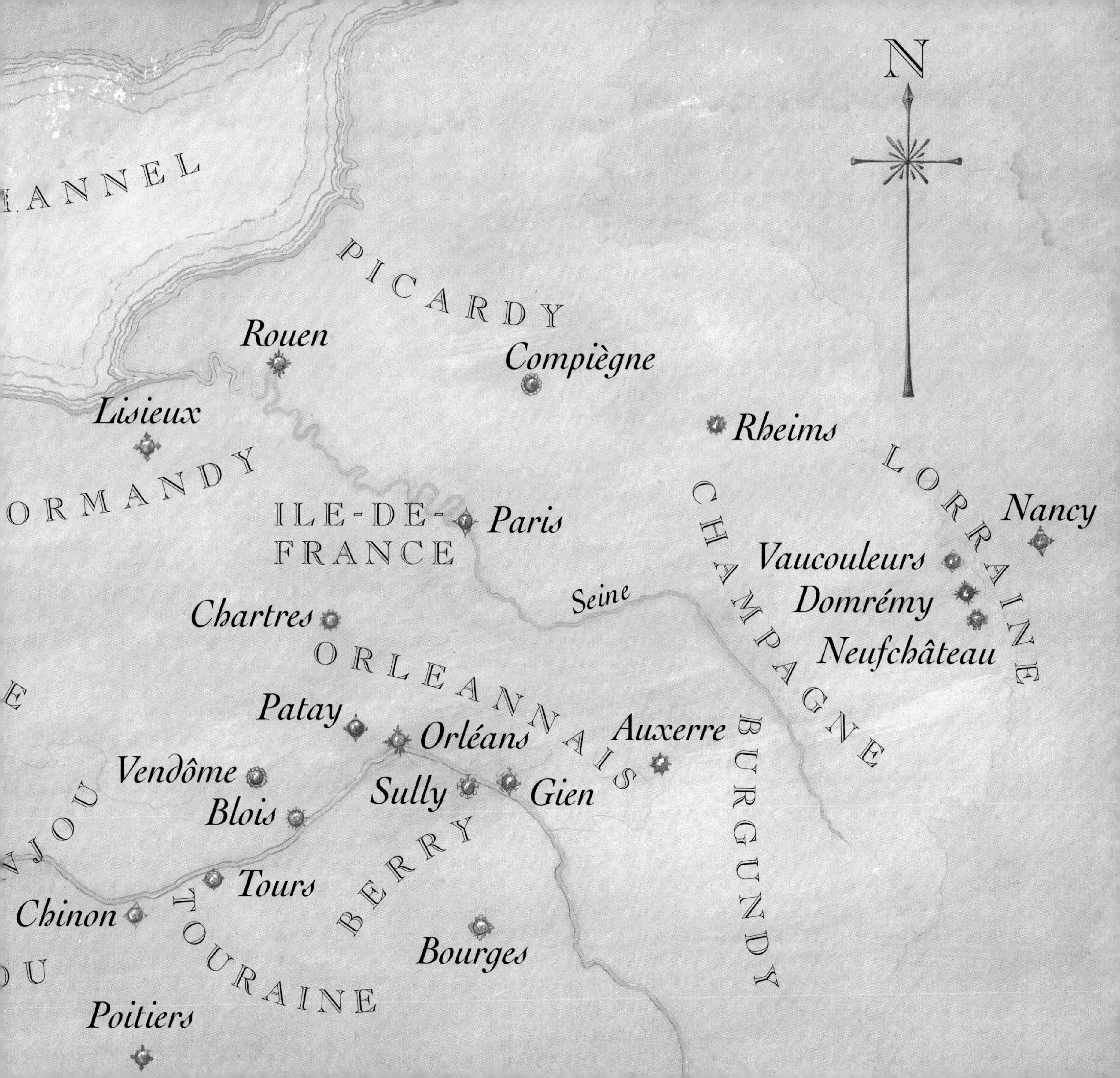

N

CHANNEL

PICARDY

Rouen

Compiègne

Lisieux

Rheims

NORMANDY

LORRAINE

Nancy

ILE-DE-
FRANCE

Paris

Vaucouleurs

CHAMPAGNE

Domrémy

Seine

Chartres

Neufchâteau

ORLEANNAIS

Patay

Auxerre

Orléans

BURGUNDY

Vendôme

Sully

Gien

ANJOU

Blois

BERRY

Tours

TOURAINE

Chinon

Bourges

Poitiers